The Myth of Balance
Published by Orange, a division of The reThink Group, Inc.
5870 Charlotte Lane, Suite 300
Cumming, GA 30040 U.S.A.
The Orange logo is a registered trademark of The reThink Group, Inc.

All Scripture quotations, unless otherwise noted, are taken from the *Holy Bible, New International Version®. NIV®.* Copyright © 1973, 1978, 1984 by International Bible Society. Used by permission of Zondervan.

Other Orange products are available online and direct from the publisher. Visit our website at www.OrangeBooks.com for more resources like these.

ISBN: 978-1-63570-901-8

Author: Frank Bealer
Lead Editor: Mike Jeffries
Art Direction: Nate Brandt
Book Design & Layout: Jacob Hunt

Printed in the United States of America
First Edition 2017

1 2 3 4 5 6 7 8 9 10

04/20/17

THE MYTH OF
BALANCE

ENDORSEMENTS

"From the time I met Frank while he was a key leader at Elevation Church, I knew he had a different energy. Not only is he off-the-charts creative, he's also a planner and strategist. He's a strong leader of people, and a purposeful dad for his kids. He and Jessica have put together a remarkable way to give priority to what matters most. But I'll let you read that for yourself in this book.

Reggie Joiner
CEO Orange / reThink Group

"Getting to work with Frank these last few years has been one of my favorite parts of being connected to ReThink. Why? Because Frank knows what it takes to build a life worth living, both at home and at work. I've benefitted from hearing about these ideas first hand, I think you'll love them too."

Jon Acuff
New York Times bestselling author of *Do Over*

"From the moment I met Frank I knew he was different. The unique thing wasn't his high energy. Though it is high! He is a dreamer for sure. The ideas that come out of his head are overwhelming to say the least. The unique thing about Frank, however, is that all of those ideas were actually being put into action and moving toward completion. If you have ever been frustrated that you can't start, continue, or finish bringing your dreams and ideas into reality, you need to hear what Frank has to say. This book is for you."

Tom Shefchunas
Middle School Pastor, North Point Community Church

"As a preacher's kid, I know what life can be like growing up in the church. I've known plenty of PKs who walked away from the church as a result. This is why it was so important for Wendy and me to have our kids not just like church, but love it. This meant making sure that they never saw the Church as competing for our time with them. If you've been in ministry for any length of time, you know this is easier said than done. This is why I think this book is so important. Jessica and Frank Bealer walk the walk. They are raising a great family and helping lead a vibrant ministry. This is a practical, how-to book that shows you how to do both. Imagine a world where ministry kids grow up loving and serving the church, and knowing how loved and valued they are by their parents. That's a strong win. This book leads you there."

Jeff Henderson
Lead Pastor, Gwinnett Church

"This great book gave me powerful and practical baby steps I could take this month to be the mom and minister I want to be. Thank you, Frank, for giving us a resource that helps us intentionally live out the priorities that we long for, and that God intends for us."

Kara Powell
PhD, Executive Director of the Fuller Youth Institute and Youth and Family Strategist for Orange

"If there is anybody that can speak more into the tension of balance in ministry, family, and devotional life it's Frank Bealer. He has managed it so well and I know as you read this book you will find the insight you need to rise higher in your life and ministry."

Craig Johnson
Sr. Director of Ministries, Lakewood Church

"I've been waiting on this book for over three years when I first heard Frank speak on this subject. This book is going to help a lot of leaders and their families. I love Frank Bealer he's the real deal. I learn from him every time I'm around him. I can't to share it with the leaders I coach."

Jim Wideman
Children's ministry pioneer, author, and Kidmin Coach

"What Frank has here is something everyone needs to read. Balancing expectations and preparation is key for anyone living in today's fast-paced society, and I believe gracing ourselves with room for interruptions is indispensable to a healthy and happy life."

Jarrid Wilson
Pastor, author of *Jesus Swagger* and *Love Is Oxygen*

"Ministry rarely fits into a 9-5 Monday to Friday schedule. There are always going to be exceptions to even the most stringent work-life boundaries. Frank Bealer has written an important book for every ministry staff member and volunteer who wants to follow in the steps of Jesus, while not missing the stops of Jesus along the way."

Dave Adamson
North Point social media and online pastor, author of *Chasing The Light*

THE MYTH OF
BALANCE

Thriving in the tension of ministry, work, and life

FRANK BEALER

TABLE OF CONTENTS

FOREWORD

People ask me all the time how I get everything done—work full time, write a blog, host two podcasts, speak at conferences, write books and have a solid marriage and make time for my now-grown kids.

But before I finish any attempt at an answer, I inevitably tell them to study Frank Bealer. If they think I get a lot done and still have a life, well, they need to meet Frank.

Frank is one of the most productive and effective leaders I've encountered. He's also one of the kindest people I know. (You can appreciate what a rare combination that is.) He always has time for me, and his family, and his friends. He soared at his incredible responsibilities at Elevation Church and as CEO of the Phase Learning Centre and Executive Director for Leadership Development at Orange.

In *The Myth of Balance*, Frank shares the secret of how he gets everything done. And it's not what you expect. I'd actually never heard of the formula Frank shares until he shared it with me. And man, I wish I had known about it when my kids were younger.

If you're tired of the pressure of work and life creating constant losses in your life, Frank's approach will be a life-saver. You really can turn the pressure into a win for everyone. I know that's a big statement, but read on. Your kids will thank you. Your wife will thank you. Your colleagues will thank you. And years from now when you look back on your life, you'll be grateful you discovered this little formula that changed so much.

Carey Nieuwhof
Founding Pastor, Connexus Church

CHAPTER 1
The Mythical Beast of Balance

I never believed in mythical beasts as a kid. You wouldn't find me searching the woods for Big Foot or scanning the ocean for the Loch Ness monster, despite all the "clear" evidence. However, for the last two decades, I've been in pursuit of perhaps the most famous mythical beast of all time. You have most likely sought it out yourself. Its attacks do not result in destruction and chaos. Instead, its deceit comes in the form of false promises. No one has ever seen it, but it keeps us all awake at night. It goes by many names but this beast is known by one name above all others: BALANCE. It lives somewhere between unemployment and renowned success. I've heard stories of encounters, but even those who claim to have beheld its wonder have been foiled by its unpredictable instability.

I'm convinced our mythical creature is of the male persuasion because it can't commit for the long term and often disengages when things get complicated. Yet just the idea that something so appealing could be yours is enough for most of us to throw caution to the wind and chase the seemingly unattainable.

The bad news is BALANCE doesn't exist. It's no more real than the Yeti. If you're like me, you've been chasing this fable for most of your adult life. At times I found it nearly in my grasp, but then it was gone again before I could even boast of my accomplishment. In the past when I've expressed my disbelief to others, their reply is one of two very extreme responses. They either adamantly insist that BALANCE does exist, or they admit through their own failed attempts that BALANCE is nothing more than a figment of the imagination

My primary testing ground for balance has been ministry in a church. My wife and I became part of a church staff soon after we were married, and the early days of matrimony and ministry gave us more than enough chances to try to capture balance. More than just proving elusive, even attempting to force balance in our lives led to as much tension as the imbalance itself did.

Here's how my wife, Jess, remembers it:

I married my high school sweetheart. He was the lead guitarist in a local band, two years older than me, a rebel with a cause, and he was hopelessly in love with me. I felt the same way. At the age of 19 I stood before God, friends, and family and promised to love him forever. We were practically kids when we recited our vows. We literally grew up together. In the 16 years we've been married, we've traveled the world, changed jobs a half dozen times, lived in four states, flipped eight houses, had three children, adopted a fourth, fought off a debilitating disease, and clearly heard the call to full-time ministry, which required a 70% pay decrease. Of all that we've experienced, the call to ministry was by far the most challenging, and it wasn't because of the reduction in our finances.

Frank and I say it all the time, MINISTRY IS MESSY! A life in ministry means talking a teen through suicidal thoughts at 2 a.m. It means cutting your date night short to rush to the hospital to comfort parents whose child has fallen ill. It means attending half a dozen graduation ceremonies in the spring, and personalizing a million Christmas cards during the holidays. Your ministry can and will take over your life.

For too many years, Frank and I struggled to balance our home life with our call to ministry. We tried to explain our busyness to our kids and justify our decisions through a lens of grace. God sacrificed everything for us, so shouldn't we be willing to give Him our all? The answer to that question is a resounding, "Yes!" But what does it mean to "give Him our all?"

A few years ago, Frank came home from the church offices pretty late, around 9 p.m. I was sitting at the bar in our kitchen trying to keep my eyes open as I edited a large-group script for our children's ministry. I had put my two little ones to bed and rented a movie to entertain my oldest so I could play catch-up on some ministry deadlines. The problem…this had been our family's pattern for about three weeks straight. Frank looked at me and said, "I don't think this is what God meant for us. Something has to give. What are we doing?" I remember replying, "Well, when you find a recipe for ministry and family, I'll be the first to drink the Kool-Aid."

God never intended for us to sacrifice the family He blessed us with on the altar of the ministry He called us to.

Little did I know how he would rise to that challenge. Frank got to work on a formula to live by. This new approach to a life in ministry helped to establish guidelines and solutions for the unexpected. It set clear boundaries and expectations. It showed us that balance is nothing more than a myth, but there's something even better.

At first, it seemed balance would be the equilibrium our young lives in ministry, family and business endeavors. But trying to achieve balance is more than a fool's errand. Making balance the goal distracts from having a plan when things inevitably go out of balance.

A life of ministry can be fulfilling without being all-consuming. God never intended for us to sacrifice the family He blessed us with on the altar of the ministry He called us to.

God didn't instill in you the desires of your heart to then compress them with a destiny that feels more like a burden. Maybe that's why the word BALANCE doesn't even appear in the Bible.

However, Jesus *did* say, "I have come that they may have life, and have it to the full." I don't think He was talking about the crazy life we often try to navigate. There is a full life in store for each of us. A life full of blessing and hope, but it's not found in balance. While balance may not be an option, I've discovered a tool to better embrace this full life. I call it "When This, Then That." Before I began to use the formula we'll talk about throughout this book, I first had to make sure my heart and mind were open and willing to try something new.

CHAPTER 2
Tell me something I don't know

Every time I enter the airport terminal I'm filled with anticipation and adventure. I love flying, at least *most* things about flying. You won't hear me complaining about long lines, the TSA or even canceled flights. But each time they make me "turn off all of my electronic devices" while they give me safety instructions, I get frustrated. How many times do I need to hear how to use a seatbelt and a life preserver? They say flying is safer than driving and no one is asking me to read a safety card before starting my car each morning. So the way I figure it, I don't need these flight instructions either.

Recently, I got on my tenth flight in a month and within moments the flight attendants gave me the evil eye as, once again, they started to offer the usual safety lesson. What they didn't understand was that I was watching a perfectly good episode from season one of *Seinfeld* on my iPad. I reluctantly removed my headphones and sat impatiently as they said something "important." I guess my countenance was communicating my frustration because let's just say my service that day was less than friendly.

Let me be clear before I start receiving corrective tweets, I know the information is important, it's just that I've heard it all before. And honestly, I don't feel like I will ever need it. In the typical book, this would be where someone would share a story of near-disaster and a new appreciation for these safety lessons. But not here. No near-death experiences. Yet.

Which is my point.

We all know ministry can be very challenging and there is potential for disaster in our lives due to the pace we run. But there's also potential for tremendous success, amazing adventure, transformed lives. Who wants to slow down when that's where the race is taking us?

We don't want to slow down, so we often choose to ignore the warnings and the people in our lives who are telling us to watch out for a potential catastrophe.

I have felt the constant pull that puts us in this difficult place nearly every day. It wasn't long ago that we were preparing for a ten-night revival when I was part of the ministry staff at Elevation Church in Charlotte. Our team couldn't have been more excited and I was filled with anticipation as my role was to make sure all of our guest speakers and artists were taken care of. This meant long days and nights. We're all used to those in ministry, but I had the extra variable of failing health. You see, I have an autoimmune disease that was in a full-on attack as revival began. I pushed through. In fact, I didn't even tell anyone what was going on because I thought it was best not to burden everyone else with my problems. I didn't want to let Jesus and everyone else down. As I type this, I realize how absolutely ridiculous this sounds.

Jess, my wife, kept telling me to call the doctor but it wasn't until everyone started asking me what was wrong that I took it seriously. This may sound extreme but it's what we do in ministry at times. We push everything to the back burner in the name of faithfulness.

We don't want to slow down, so we often choose to ignore the warnings and the people in our lives who are telling us to watch out for a potential catastrophe.

We divert these warnings by calling it a "busy season," which is often just another way of saying life is going to be a roller coaster for the next few months so everybody hold on because I *think* it will end safely. We often excuse our mismanagement of time, energy, and effort as just being busy. But as my friend Mike Foster, founder of People of the Second Chance, likes to say, "You're ridiculously in charge of your own life!"

We can't operate as though our calling is temporary.

I've learned that without making shifts in the way we lead and manage our lives, we are not going to be in ministry for the long haul.

We can't operate as though our calling is temporary.

We have Hebrews to thank for that reminder. "And let us run with endurance the race God has set before us." (Hebrews 12:1)

For most of us, our calling to ministry is designed to last a lifetime. So why do half of all people in vocational ministry give up in less than five years?

I have never had to take advantage of those aircraft safety instructions, but that doesn't mean the danger isn't real. In the movie *Sully*, about the water landing in the Hudson River, I saw something I never knew about flight attendants. In the event of a crash landing, they are trained to say a phrase loudly, over and over again in unison. "Brace, brace, brace! Heads down, stay down. Brace, brace, brace! Heads down, stay down." This is a last-ditch effort to prepare everyone for what's in store. If the passengers weren't listening or they begin to panic or they were watching Seinfeld on their iPad, at least they'll hear this: "Brace, brace, brace! Heads down, stay down. Brace, brace, brace! Heads down, stay down."

Consider this book my attempt to do just that. You may have ignored every warning sign or piece of advice by wise leaders up until this point but I hope you hear me say **"Make plans today for what lies ahead. Don't give up, there's too much at stake!"**

QUICK ASSESSMENT

You may wonder how you can know you need to make some changes. After all, the warning signs don't come in the form of sirens and flashing lights but they are still present. Start with these questions.

ASK YOURSELF:

How long can I sustain my current pace?

Am I feeling underappreciated?

How much sleep have I been getting?

Has my devotional life been on the decline?

ASK YOUR FRIENDS/FAMILY:

When I'm with you, do you feel like I'm fully present?

What changes have you seen in me?

What is the hardest part of my role in ministry?

CHAPTER 3
Problems when we say 'they'

One of the biggest indicators that things are starting to get sideways in your life is in the language that you use. No, I'm not talking about profanity, although that may indicate other issues. I've narrowed it down to two big categories. There's what you say to *friends and family* and there's what you are saying about the *leadership of the church*.

Let's start with *friends and family*. A few years ago, I was at the office late one evening when I discovered there was another meeting I needed to attend that night. This is normally not a big deal but the fact that I had already been away three nights that week and I had already committed to a night of wrestling on the floor with my kids was the problem. Let me be clear, the meeting wasn't the problem. My poor planning was.

The idea of picking up the phone to call my wife and kids to say "I'm sorry" again simply wasn't acceptable. I had been saying "I'm sorry" a lot lately and there had started to be rumblings in our house, and not the fun rough-housing "Let's Get Ready to Rumble" kind. The church was taking too much time. We were all feeling it. On this particular night, I realized that their recent frustration with the church and ministry had nothing to do with them or the church but had everything to do with me. There had been a time when exceptions to the schedule would come up and I would give vision to it to make it a positive. I would say things like "we get to" and "this is so important because," but I had gotten lazy and it's hard to say those things when you say them all of the time. A language shift had occurred and everyone felt it. It wasn't until I took responsibility for how I was managing my life and how I communicated that things began to change. It only took me about a decade in ministry to figure this out.

Until we take responsibility, we will continue to pursue balance and blame others when we can't find it.

Then there's the way you talk about the leadership of the church. Have you shifted from saying "we" to saying "they" when you talk about leadership decisions in the church?

It's a subtle change from "we" to "they" and yet it's extremely poisonous.

Last year, a young man approached me after a session at Orange Conference to ask a few questions about a talk I had just done on Leading Up. We decided to walk to get a coffee and chat. He took out a pen and paper eager to learn. He asked, "How do you change their mind, when they decide to put on an event that will put an excessive burden on my volunteers?" I asked a couple of clarifying questions, hoping to give him some good advice. He continued, "I just don't feel like they understand children's ministry. They always fail to think about us." There it was again! I think he was expecting me to give five easy steps for leading up. Instead I stopped, got on my figurative soap box and delivered a homily on language and ownership. You see, leading change is very difficult when you declare division in the church. Whatever your role is at the church, you have ownership and responsibility for the decisions that are made. Instead of saying "they" don't understand children's ministry, it's better for us to say "we" have a lot to learn on how to ensure that all of our ministry teams are in alignment.

I know what you may be thinking. How is saying "I'm sorry" and "they" a real indicator that my life is a mess? Language often reflects what is going on in our heart.

Matthew 12:34b says, "For the mouths speaks what the heart is full of."

If we maintain an unhealthy perspective, it will be too easy to blame our life management problems on the church and the ministry. Until we take responsibility, we will continue to pursue balance and blame others when we can't find it.

The great news is that a healthy approach to ministry is available and it's not just subject to where we work and who we work for. Ultimately, we can take ownership in how we operate our lives.

CHAPTER 4
Get out of the clouds

At this point, I may have successfully increased your stress by highlighting the tensions you are already experiencing. The good news is that tension can be good. Now change can begin. There is hope.

I've often found that my "to do" list outnumbers the hours in a day, and it's difficult to know where to begin. Expectation weighs heavily, and no matter how many times I check my calendar, rework my schedule, or request a deadline extension, life seems to spiral out of control.

It's an endless cycle. My unrealistic schedule leads to unmet expectations, which leads to worry about my job, my family's security, and those I serve. I determine to pick up the pace. I add more to my schedule, fail once again, and then worry yet again about the consequences. But wait...I'll just pick up the pace!

And so the cycle continues.

Worry often feels like a big black cloud hanging over our head. And no, I'm not referring to the mysterious place in the sky where our emails and music live. I'm talking about the fear of failure, the disillusionment of doubt, and the weariness of worry. They float

above, constantly looming, casting a shadow on even bright and shiny moments. For the sake of the illustration, let's call those bright moments rainbows. How many rainbows have you disregarded because surviving the torrential rains was all the burden you could bear?

For change to occur, we must get rid of the cloud.

Recently I tried to explain this to my 14-year-old son.

Here is the question I posed. "Imagine you make a $1,000 per month (he instantly thought he was rich!), but you have no budget. You know approximately how much money you need to live on, but it's getting close to the end of the month, and a couple of bills haven't been paid yet. Your friend invites you to an NBA game. Here's the kicker. They are incredible seats and it's only going to cost you $100. Should you go?"

Micah responded enthusiastically, "Yes! Wait...how much do I owe in other bills?"

I answered, "I'm not sure exactly. I think you'll have enough, but you might be a little short on your bills if you go to the game."

And here comes the proud dad moment. Micah squinted his eyes in thought and said, "Why wouldn't I just write it all down and figure it out?"

His response was logical. Most of us would answer the same way in this scenario, but for some reason, we don't approach worry with the same logic and rationale. We say, "I'm so busy today. I don't know if I can get it all done." What does that even mean? You've set self-imposed expectations for yourself that you aren't even sure are possible. It's a maddening existence.

Our biggest challenge, when it comes to productivity, is knowing WHAT needs to be done WHEN. You will always

Just because you FEEL overwhelmed doesn't mean your work schedule is paralyzing you. Feelings are not always a reflection of the truth.

struggle to find fulfillment in a life of ministry, to identify those rainbows with everything floating like a black cloud above your head. At some point, the storm will be too much. You'll hear the roll of thunder, the crack of lightning, and you'll throw your hands to the sky in surrender because uncertainty and the risk of collapse is the worse kind of stress. If that's where you are, if it feels like you're standing in the middle of Tropical Storm (Insert Your Name), it's time to stop. Cancel your subscription to the cloud. (See what I did there?). It's impossible to eliminate stress entirely, but by identifying WHAT is causing you to feel overwhelmed and acknowledging WHEN it has to be completed, you control the forecast.

Thankfully, this doesn't necessarily call for a complete turnaround or change of lifestyle. It just means you call it like you see it. You label it. You acknowledge individually every agenda item that must be completed and you realistically set a timeline. Before your day begins, look at those items designated as a "must do." Your list may look something like this: five phone calls, nine emails, three meetings, and one project.

Just because you FEEL overwhelmed doesn't mean your work schedule is paralyzing you. Feelings are not always a reflection of the truth.

This may seem obvious, but until we take time to write down what we know to be true about our schedule, it will be impossible to prepare for the actual challenges our schedule will bring.

This small change is worth your time and effort. It's easy to become burdened by the details, but by remembering who you are fighting for (your spouse, your kids, your friends, and the families you serve) it makes the effort worthwhile. Your emotional health is directly dependent on your ability to manage the details of your daily schedule. You only get one shot at this whirlwind life. Don't allow the funnel to devour your carefully laid out plans because you were distracted by the color of Dorothy's shoes.

(Don't worry. I know you don't always see the storm coming. We'll cover that after this exercise.)

Before you move on to the next chapter, take a few minutes to work on your priorities. Put them in an order that shows their importance to you. After you have created your list, compare it to last week's calendar. For most of us, we will see that many of our top priorities receive the least amount of our time.

CHAPTER 5
Pardon the exceptions

If the schedule in ministry isn't the real challenge, what is? One word: Exceptions. After all, ministry is all about exceptions.

Exceptions are the things that come up after your calendar is scheduled for the week. Exceptions are messy.

These exceptions are the people that need our love, care, and shepherding. It's the 30-minute call that turns into an hour, the unexpected hospital visit, the emergency meeting because a vendor isn't going to be able to meet your deadline. This is the very essence of ministry. And yet it's the very thing that makes our lives complicated.

Without the exceptions that come up, aiming for balance while in ministry might be attainable. Clock in. Do your work, and clock out just like at many other jobs. But ministry involves lots of people on different levels: the families you serve, the volunteers you lead, and the staff you partner with. People make ministry messy. When their lives spiral out of control, they call you. Suddenly, their dilemma becomes yours. It's not a bad thing that people turn to the church when they need help. It's exactly how God intended it to be, but it does make for a lot of exceptions. The hard thing about exceptions is that they never happen when it's convenient for us. What are we to do?

Here are a few approaches to exceptional interruptions:

The Always Open Approach

You could simply leave so much margin in your day for whatever may occur. You may be completely ineffective in your day-to-day routine but when something comes up, you will respond very quickly. I can see it now, your pastor walks up and says "What are you going to do today?" and you respond "Oh, I don't know. Whatever the Lord brings my way." Let me know how that works out for you.

The Highly-Caffeinated Approach

You run as fast as you can for as long as you can, collecting all kinds of medals for the first few laps of the race. You may crash one day but that's probably not a big deal as long as you are okay finding yourself on the ground as a broken leader who's not very effective in leading your church or ministry in the near future. (This is the most common approach.)

The Snappy Approach

You resign yourself to a life of frustration and stressful conversations with your spouse and friends as you struggle through the impossible schedule of ministry. These conversations require you to find a way to explain again why this thing is just as important as the last thing that kept you away from the things that matter most.

As you will soon discover, this is my favorite. This approach allows you to acknowledge the tensions in ministry and leaves room for many important things to be happening in your life at the same time.

The When This Then That Approach

As my wife and I have pursued our calling in ministry over the last twenty years, we have learned a lot about what it looks like for our family to be in ministry together. We want to serve Jesus with all that we have and that requires planning and changes. We have decided that exceptions may make ministry complicated but they don't make it impossible.

You probably already have guidelines for governing your life. These might be intentional or unintentional, spoken or unspoken, written on the wall or scattered in the hall. But everyone knows some guidelines exist: From how often you text at the dinner table, to how much you talk on your phone in the car, to how the laundry gets washed, to how frequently you open your computer at night to do just a "little more work."

Guidelines are extremely helpful, but those guidelines will turn into a squiggly mess when confronted with important but unexpected exceptions. This is where we can all improve.

As I see it, there are two types of exceptions: "If Exceptions" and "When Exceptions."

Exceptions may make ministry complicated but they don't make it impossible.

If Exceptions are challenging circumstances that don't happen that often. Can you imagine trying to plan for every possible challenging scenario that could come up in ministry? Me neither. There are going to be some things that we could never plan or prepare for. We could spend our whole lives worrying about the what ifs in our calendar, but that doesn't seem very practical or helpful.

When Exceptions, on the other hand, are things that aren't on your schedule but you know they are going to come up because they happen with some measure of frequency. They might be a little unexpected, but they're the unexpected exceptions we know to expect.

We've learned that embracing the idea that ministry is exceptions changes everything.

I'm convinced that if we were better at handling the When Exceptions, then our ministries could be greatly improved.

Over time, Jess and I have learned how to better communicate when unexpected exceptions arise. But the solution extends beyond healthy communication. A life in ministry is so unique that it needs its own language, especially when faced with the dilemma of all those exceptions.

We've learned that embracing the idea that ministry is exceptions changes everything.

Because it is not a matter of IF exceptions will happen it's a matter of WHEN.

CHAPTER 6
Do that when: Dessert Edition

Do you remember the first time you asked someone if they liked you? Like in elementary school? Or maybe like me, middle school? More than likely it didn't happen instantly. You thought about it. A lot. You played through all kinds of scenarios in your mind.

Recently, my kids came across my old middle school yearbooks. They started asking all kinds of questions, mostly around haircuts and fashion but at some point it drifted to what one girl wrote in the back of my yearbook. It was an old girlfriend. Sheesh! They asked how long we dated and how I asked her out. I explained how easy it was. I handed her a note that said, "Do you like me? Check yes or no on the inside." They laughed, a lot. I shot back by asking, "Well, what's your plan?" One of our teenagers said, "Oh, I just ask to borrow their phone for a minute and text myself. Now, I have their number. A little later I just start texting with them." Like that's the most obvious thing in the world. Honestly, I was half-disturbed and half-proud. At least he had a plan.

We need a plan. The idea of having a strategy for work and family isn't new and yet it's strange that every day we get up, head to work, and know we are probably going to fall short. Still, we aren't making a change.

The danger for not applying a strategy toward our work schedules is huge. The arguments grow. The stress builds and kids start to see a messier side of ministry. Parameters aren't clear. Goals aren't set. Friends are lost. Vacations get bumped or misappropriated. The next thing you know, you're sitting by the ocean with friends and start thinking this is the perfect time to get caught up on a few things because time off becomes time to check off something on your to-do list.

Just because ministry is filled with exceptions doesn't mean we have to be surprised.

What else can you do? There's work to be done and if you don't get it done, who will?

Since it's impossible to fit everything that happens on your 9-5 calendar (which doesn't actually exist anyway), what will you do when things come up?

The exceptions to your schedule are already in motion. There's no way to avoid them. Your plans will change in a moment. People will need you and it won't fit into your schedule. You got into ministry to respond to the needs of others. So why is there so little time for them?

Just because ministry is filled with exceptions doesn't mean we have to be surprised. It has always intrigued me how many people continue to be caught off-guard by the inevitable.

Every Christmas, our family likes to watch *Elf*. There is a scene where over-sized elf Will Ferrell is assigned the horrible task of checking to make sure each jack in the box is working properly. He turns the crank and the clown pops out. He is startled every time it happens. It's a funny moment in the movie. What's not so funny is that many of us are living our lives turning the crank but not prepared for what's next.

A couple of times each year, most churches do a big push to get people connected to a small group. At our church, any member of our

staff could tell you about when it's going to happen. New participants would typically sign up before they went to get their kids and it would always take a few minutes to find the right small group for their schedule. This meant that our children's ministry would be watching kids a little longer on those weekends. Every time, a couple of our staff members would be caught off-guard by this. Small-group sign ups were a pretty normal part of our schedule, but immediately the weekend would be thrown off. Compare that to the veterans who determined not to be surprised by these weekends of different programming. When they planned for the exception, it became an opportunity to shine.

These leaders would coordinate fun games and order pizza for all of the volunteers that are spending extra time at church. Now, instead of stressed-out kids that are ready to go home, these volunteers and parents discover they have well-fed, happy kids and everybody is ready for a Sunday afternoon nap.

Exceptions become incredible opportunities. Opportunities to care for those in need. Opportunities to use your training and skills to help someone. Opportunities to integrate your family and friends in your calling.

Over the years, I had the incredible privilege of interviewing people looking to join the staff at Elevation Church. This required my wife and I to go to dinner with prospective couples. Great for the interview process, but it was challenging to tie up another night away from the kids. We knew that getting out of the office environment to a nice restaurant was the best way to hear what people were thinking and to answer any questions that they may have.

Some seasons involved more interviews than others, but about two years ago it started to get crazy. The church was growing radically and there were so many candidates to meet. This required flexibility and therefore led to a multitude of unplanned exceptions.

I'm sure you see where this is heading. You've been there. If you are like me, I was trying to limit my nights away from family to no more than three nights a week but those were on the calendar (no room for surprises). These interview dinners meant a fourth or maybe even fifth night away from home.

WHEN we have an interview, THEN the kids get to eat at the restaurant (at a separate table) with an appetizer and dessert.

I found that when I would call home to tell my kids that I wouldn't be home because I had an interview, it would be met with massive disappointment but then a sweet little smile saying, "We love you Daddy. It's okay. I was just really hoping we could play a board game tonight." My heart would break.

We needed a plan. This is where "When This Then That" comes into play.

The interviews weren't going to stop. And my kids weren't going anywhere.

So, we made a shift. When I had an opportunity to do another interview for the church, I would call home to say we have an interview (same as before), but instead of this meaning Mom and Dad wouldn't be home, it meant an adventure for the kids. We created a new When This Then That solution. WHEN we have an interview, THEN the kids get to eat at the restaurant (at a separate table) with an appetizer and dessert.

If you have kids, you know this is a really big deal. I don't know about you but when we take our family to a restaurant, we try to be extremely efficient. We get in. We get out. Before the chaos ensues. We don't order appetizers. We order our drinks and meal at the exact same time and we rarely order dessert. After all, how can we ask our kids to behave when we give them tons of sugar and then keep them trapped in a booth?

Can you imagine the change this made for our family? Instead of sadness, our phone calls were met with jubilee.

You can see how we were able to turn something that used to be a negative, another 'I'm sorry' into something that our whole family gets excited about. In fact, sometimes my kids ask when the next interview is so they can dine out "fancy" again.

When guidelines are clear and solutions are created in advance, serving in the local church becomes an empowering way of life, not a sacrificial burden to bear.

Family and ministry can be done well. I've seen many examples of healthy families creating solutions instead of trying to achieve the impossible feat of balance. When guidelines are clear and solutions are created in advance, serving in the local church becomes an empowering way of life, not a sacrificial burden to bear.

Desserts or not, I don't want to imply that Jess and I have it all figured out. We are, however, trying to be strategic and honest about what it looks like for our ministry to be a family calling, not just a personal one.

Before we move forward, take a minute to write out one When This Then That solution. (You will use it as part of an exercise in the next chapter.)

CHAPTER 7
Recipe for disaster

If you aren't careful, even the best of these solutions can be a recipe for disaster. There are key elements that must be considered.

Jess and I learned this the hard way. Our approach seemed like a good idea at the time, but it turned out to be a flawed solution. It went like this: "When we have to miss one of our kid's athletic events, then we will get a play-by-play reenactment later that night." It was a really fun idea, but quickly created problems with missed bedtimes and late nights and exhausted parents. We made one simple change and this one went from a mess to something more manageable. The new solution: When we have to miss one of our kids' athletic events, then we have a play-by-play recap via Facetime.

Over time, I've discovered six keys to a great When This Then That solution.

ONE: THE "WHEN" OCCURS RANDOMLY BUT OFTEN.
It can be really difficult to experience the benefits of a great solution when you never get to try it. My wife has three cookbooks. We received all of them when we got married. I think I've eaten one meal from those recipes. I'm sure they are filled with all kinds of sweet

and savory dishes but I will never know because they are currently on top of our kitchen cabinets underneath a decorative dish. Make sure that the solutions you create have a *when* that you know is going to happen. It would be a waste of time for me to create a solution like this: When my wife cooks a gourmet dish from the cookbook, I will buy her a dozen roses. It's just never going to happen.

TWO: "THIS" IS SPECIFIC.

Be as specific as possible. General statements here can get you in trouble. If you have a weak "This" then your "That" becomes optional (which means it probably will not happen).

A friend of mine would always say, "When I work late, then I will leave early the next day." What is late? When is the line crossed? How do I hold myself accountable to late? A better way would be to say, "When I work past 6:45 p.m., I will make an arrangement to leave by 5 p.m. one of the following two days." Remember, the whole reason to create these solutions is to have a predictable plan when unpredictable things happen.

THREE: IT TAKES DELIBERATE ACTION.

Not only does the *when* have to happen, but the *that* has to happen too. You have to do your part. Creating a bunch of solutions that don't actually happen is going to frustrate everyone. You can't control the *when*, but you can control the *that*. If you start making exceptions for your solutions then the whole strategy unravels. You have to be fully committed that you can and will complete the *that*.

A friend of ours created a When This Then That solution for her roommates. When I don't get all my work done during the day, then I ask my roommates if they have any work to do and we will work together at a coffee shop to ensure we are still spending time together even in the midst of busy weeks. She recognized that sometimes work just can't stop, but that she could have a plan to make sure relationships stayed strong. Can you imagine how lame it would have been if she told her roommates about her stay-connected strategy but never followed through?

FOUR: IT TAKES ACCOUNTABILITY.

Once you have clearly defined the *this*, you must follow through on your new plan. Share your new solutions with a few close friends or mentors to make follow-through fun and real.

Carey Nieuwhof is one of the wisest men I know. He's great at creating a plan and completing it. When my family schedule flipped upside down with a change of jobs, relocation to a new city, and the addition of a newly adopted teenager to our home, I called Carey to help me stay on track. He never lets a phone call go by without checking on my efforts to keep family and ministry healthy.

Once you complete your solutions, share them with someone who will follow up. It's not enough to just share them. You must share them with someone who is invested enough in your life to see that they actually happen.

FIVE: IT MUST BE HELPFUL.

Don't create a solution that makes things more difficult.

Example: When I don't make it home for dinner with the family, I will take them to dinner the next night.

This one is difficult because it's nearly impossible to commit to. I'm already behind. What if another exception comes up? What if your entire family can't be there the next night or having dinner together means a 15-minute Taco Bell run where everyone stuffs their face because it doesn't fit the schedule? This solution feels impossible and only serves to make life more difficult and chaotic. Make sure you're not digging a deeper hole.

SIX: SET YOURSELF UP FOR SUCCESS.

After I shared the When This Then That strategy with my friend Jon Torres, he came up with one of his own. I'll let him describe it:

> Being in ministry means hearing horror stories about ministry leaders' kids who end up hating the church. I mean, why wouldn't they? The church is taking mommy or daddy all day (and some-

49

times at night) without even so much as a thank you. I noticed my own two young boys start to deflate anytime I had to tell them I had to go back into the office after a short dinner visit. My gut-wrenching moment came as I watched my four-year-old try to explain to my two-year-old that Daddy had to leave because other people needed him more.

Something had to change.

My sons are really big fans of toys. Who knew!? So when I noticed that the grocery store was having a sale on Hot Wheels cars, I bought a bunch and filled my desk with them. Now anytime I have to stay late, I come home with a couple of Hot Wheels and a "thank you" card written by me, but from my church and from my lead pastor. Why my lead pastor? Because I don't want my kids to resent my boss any more than I want them to resent the church; they often go hand-in-hand.

Being prepared for late nights has changed my life as a father. If I come home late now, I've shown love to my family by being prepared for it. It has now been transformed from "stealing daddy" to a moment of expressed gratitude to my kids (who still love toys) from my "work."

My When This Then That solution: When I need to work late on a project with our senior staff, then I bring home a special treat from my lead pastor and the church to let them know they are never taken for granted.

BONUS: NO ANDS OR BUTS.

These solutions are intended to be easy and clear. If we start building solutions where everything must align perfectly in order for them to happen, then nothing will change. Keep your recipes AND or BUT free.

It may take a couple of hours to make sure your When This Then That solutions meet all of the criteria mentioned here, but it's worth it.

WHO WILL YOU CHOOSE TO HOLD YOU ACCOUNTABLE?
(CIRCLE ONE)

Parent/Family Member

Fellow staff member

Mentor

Pastor

Friend

HOW OFTEN WILL YOU ASK THEM TO CHECK ON YOU?
(CIRCLE ONE)

Weekly

Biweekly

Monthly

Quarterly

CHAPTER 8
Take the leap

The first (and only time) I went bungee jumping, I climbed up the tower in Pigeon Forge, Tennessee to impress a girl. She later became my wife, so I guess it worked despite the debacle that ensued. I convinced myself that this was an incredible exhibition of my manliness and faith in God. (Give me a break. I had only been a believer for about 11 months at this point and hadn't made it to Luke chapter 4 about testing God).

After getting the harness on and walking out on the platform, my heart started to beat out of my chest. I thought I was ready but when I got up there, I realized I was in trouble. I was surprised by how high it was. I looked to the attendant and said, "Dude, can you push me?" Nope. So there I was. I determined the climb back down was more terrifying than throwing myself toward the ground attached only to a large rubber band. As I leaned forward, I realized that the guardrails wrapped all the way around and my instinct kicked in. I grabbed the rails hanging parallel to the ground and held on for dear life. Not a very cool moment, but I assure you, I'm much cooler now. I eventually let go and bounced to the big blue safety pillow below.

I had a horrible approach to bungee jumping. It's a wonder that I didn't dislocate my shoulders. Or worse, die of embarrassment!

Honestly, I have spent too much time hanging on to those rails in ministry.

If we are going to experience life in ministry to the full, we must improve our approach.

It's my hope you will take the next necessary steps to embrace the truth that ministry is exceptions but we don't have to be surprised.

Next Steps:

1. Read through some real-life When This Then That solutions from some of my friends.

2. Develop your own When This Then That scenarios and solutions on the worksheets provided.

Real-life When This Than That examples

Chris and Holly Brown

Host of the nationally syndicated radio show *Chris Brown's True Stewardship* and *The Leadership Momentum Podcast*

One rule of thumb we live by with two full-time ministry positions is, "one dunk at a time." (My wife's a basketball fan, hence the name.) Essentially what it means is: When one of us has a stretching or "dunk the ball" week, the other one has to fall back and cover the rest of the court to keep as much away from the one dunking as possible. The "dunks" can be a writing deadline, a new speaking event, launching a campus, executing a staff retreat, or one of the other major happenings that come up. You name it, but we both have them and a dunking week takes up almost all the emotional energy you have. We've learned from experience that two people dunking at the same time is miserable for the whole family. It's comparable to being asked to write an essay in a doctor's exam room with three toddlers, all while wearing a paper gown. We did that once or twice and realized if we don't get a new plan, our ministry callings or our family were going to bite the big one. So now, we communicate with each other ahead of time when a "dunk the ball" week is coming. The

57

other spouse does their absolute best not to schedule anything too emotionally taxing in that same week. Instead they become the flexible one: picking up extra roles with the kids, being willing to come home from work early or go in late as needed, making the bed in the morning, and handling the evening dishes. While one is focused and rigid in their schedule the other is scanning the court for possible problems and is flexible to handle them as they arise.

Clay Scroggins
Lead Pastor at North Point Community Church

I love the language of When This Then That. My wife and I use it when I'm coming in and out of busy seasons. Although we love date nights, we don't really have a routine of date nights. So we try to strategically plan them around busy seasons. For instance, I have some weeks where I have no weeknight events, but I have some weeks where I have two or three. When my wife and I see a busy week coming, then we make sure to plan a date night before that week and after that week. It's helpful for us to get on the same page and for her to feel connected before the whirlwind and it also gives us something to look forward to after the busy week.

Nathan McLean
Hillsong Kids Pastor

My wife and I have the incredible privilege of helping launch new Hillsong campuses all over Australia. One of our most recent launches took us to Bali, Indonesia. With our church being multi-campus, I often travel and sometimes need to be away overnight or even multiple nights. I feel it's very important that we are intentional about family time. The kids know that when Dad is away overnight with ministry, then I will always bring home a present. The longer the trip, the bigger the present. It fills our kids with a sense of anticipation and creates special opportunities for us to talk about God's faithfulness as we play with our new toys. I know it's really simple but it has been crucial to our family.

The big thing we often speak of when we give the gifts is that God isn't just using Mum and Dad but he is using our entire family to grow his church. So if Bali has a lot of salvations (which it did), I thank them for being a part of that by sharing their daddy.

Brandon Hibbard
Family Ministry Creative Director at Elevation Church

Videos are an integral part of how we teach kids and students at Elevation. The team I get to work with is incredible and they only want the best for the families of our church. Oftentimes, video shoots will go late into the night to get just the right shot. So, when I have video shoots that go into the evening, then I arrange to keep the kids a little longer the next morning. This makes the next morning less stressful for my wife, Rachel. Plus I get some kid time. Double bonus!

Kevin Monahan
Next Generation Ministry Lead at 12Stone Church

About twelve times a year, I leave my family for more than a day. From mission trips, conferences, or staff retreats, sometimes something that requires me to travel away from my family. Now any good husband discusses overnight departures with his spouse; that's just basic marriage survival. However, about five years ago, I began to invite my children into the permission phase of planning. When I get an invite to leave Atlanta, then we have a brief family meeting to discuss whether I should accept the request.

Of course, there have been rare opportunities where I have no choice but to accept, but most of the prospects are relatively optional. At first it was a bit awkward, but over the years the discussions have been vital in me determining the necessity of travel. I often get reminded of extracurricular activities that I would have easily forgotten about. Other times I have declined an invite because it wasn't best for my entire family. Questions like, "Do you want to go or do you need to go?" "Have you prayed about it, Dad?" "Will there be wifi so we can Facetime?" have now became the standard array of questions that help me make the best decisions. Leaving with permission elevates my ability to lead without division.

Rich Birch
Founder of Unseminary

My day job is running a camp in Canada ... my kids still like "snow days" in the winter but it's kinda boring for them. When there is a snow day and I'm heading to our site, then they are welcome to come with me and play in all the winter wonderland stuff we have ... sledding, skiing, etc.

Matt Guevara
Executive Director of
International Network of Children's Ministry

In certain seasons, high ministry seasons or high travel seasons, when I come home then I leave my phone and my bag in the car. I do this as a signal to let my family know: I'm here for you and there's no way I can be called away. We live in too close proximity to our devices.

Jim Wideman
Kidmin Coach

I never wanted my kids to feel like they were ever second place to the church, so Julie and I established a birthday policy that when the girls' birthday fell on a church day (Sunday or Wednesday) that they not only got to choose another day to have their parties, they got a birthday week where they got to pick what we ate that week both at home and which restaurants we ate at when we went out.

As our kids got older and had money of their own, I wanted a fun way to teach them to be generous and that Father God loves to bless His kids. Here's what I did. Anytime I needed change for a tip or for a parking meter, I asked my girls to help. If I needed a five or three ones instead of paying them back when I got change, I gave them my bigger bill. Sometimes they got a five dollars for two dollars, sometime it was a five for a twenty. I've even blessed them with larger bills with fifties and hundreds when I could. Even to this day when I ask my family anyone have three dollars or even a quarter they stop what they are doing and try to be the first to help because they know Dad wants to bless them.

WORKSHEETS

Create your own When This Then That scenarios and be sure they meet the following seven suggestions:

RANDOM BUT OFTEN

SPECIFIC

ACTIONABLE

ACCOUNTABLE

HELPFUL

SETUP FOR SUCCESS

NO ANDS OR BUTS

DOUBLE CHECK:

- ☐ Random but not often
- ☐ Specific
- ☐ Actionable
- ☐ Helpful
- ☐ Set up for success
- ☐ No and or buts

_____

_____

_____

_____

_____

_____

_____

_____

_____

_____

_____

_____

_____

_____

_____

DOUBLE CHECK:

- ☐ Random but not often
- ☐ Specific
- ☐ Actionable
- ☐ Helpful
- ☐ Set up for success
- ☐ No and or buts

DOUBLE CHECK:

- ☐ Random but not often
- ☐ Specific
- ☐ Actionable
- ☐ Helpful
- ☐ Set up for success
- ☐ No and or buts

DOUBLE CHECK:

- ■ Random but not often
- ■ Specific
- ■ Actionable
- ■ Helpful
- ■ Set up for success
- ■ No and or buts

DOUBLE CHECK:

- ☐ Random but not often
- ☐ Specific
- ☐ Actionable
- ☐ Helpful
- ☐ Set up for success
- ☐ No and or buts

DOUBLE CHECK:

- ■ Random but not often
- ■ Specific
- ■ Actionable
- ■ Helpful
- ■ Set up for success
- ■ No and or buts

DOUBLE CHECK:

- ☐ Random but not often
- ☐ Specific
- ☐ Actionable
- ☐ Helpful
- ☐ Set up for success
- ☐ No and or buts

DOUBLE CHECK:

- ☐ Random but not often
- ☐ Specific
- ☐ Actionable
- ☐ Helpful
- ☐ Set up for success
- ☐ No and or buts

72

DOUBLE CHECK:

- ■ Random but not often
- ■ Specific
- ■ Actionable
- ■ Helpful
- ■ Set up for success
- ■ No and or buts

DOUBLE CHECK:

- ☐ Random but not often
- ☐ Specific
- ☐ Actionable
- ☐ Helpful
- ☐ Set up for success
- ☐ No and or buts

74

DOUBLE CHECK:

- ■ Random but not often
- ■ Specific
- ■ Actionable
- ■ Helpful
- ■ Set up for success
- ■ No and or buts

DOUBLE CHECK:

- Random but not often
- Specific
- Actionable
- Helpful
- Set up for success
- No and or buts

DOUBLE CHECK:

- ☐ Random but not often
- ☐ Specific
- ☐ Actionable
- ☐ Helpful
- ☐ Set up for success
- ☐ No and or buts

_____

_____

_____

_____

_____

_____

_____

_____

_____

_____

_____

_____

DOUBLE CHECK:

- ☐ Random but not often
- ☐ Specific
- ☐ Actionable
- ☐ Helpful
- ☐ Set up for success
- ☐ No and or buts

DOUBLE CHECK:

- ☐ Random but not often
- ☐ Specific
- ☐ Actionable
- ☐ Helpful
- ☐ Set up for success
- ☐ No and or buts

DOUBLE CHECK:

- ☐ Random but not often
- ☐ Specific
- ☐ Actionable
- ☐ Helpful
- ☐ Set up for success
- ☐ No and or buts

**Share your
When This Then That
solutions at:**

www.mythofbalance.com